A Parent's Guide to Building Self-Esteem

taking your parenting to the next level...

By Joy Osborn & Sue Stead
Future Childcare Training Ltd

First published in the United Kingdom in 2007 by
Future Childcare Training Ltd
PO Box 4388
Rugby
Warwickshire
CV21 9DN

Future Childcare Training Limited Registered in England and Wales.
Company Registration No: 4626722.
www.FutureChildcareTraining.com

ISBN   978 0 9555260 0 8

Printed and Bound in Great Britain by
Broadleaf Graphical, Heathcote, Warwick

future
childcare training limited

Contents

A Parent's Guide to Building Self-Esteem

taking your parenting to the next level...

INTRODUCTION

When parenting children one of the most important things we can do is to build their self-esteem, in fact it is vital. 'Where do I start?' is a common response. Defining self-esteem is often difficult. We all have a good sense of what it is but no structure by which to identify or measure it. We can tell when a child's potential and capabilities are clouded by self-doubt or by lack of self-worth and sometimes we can link these feelings to the emotional scars of family life, relationships or upsets.

However, how many of us can say we are clear about how to really help when people get down? Mostly we act on instinct and knowledge that self-esteem is about building a person's confidence in themselves and their abilities. We also know that a person who has a low self-esteem will lack in feelings of significance, belonging, personal worth or competence.

Having low self-esteem will affect the way we live our lives. Sometimes people cannot move on or tackle some of their life issues because they have no confidence in themselves and cannot imagine how the future could be. What most parents want for their children is to go through life confidently and have the opportunity to get all they want out of life.

It is common for parents to worry about their child's self-esteem. This book has been created as a guide for parents. It will help with identifying a loss of self-esteem and give a structured approach to understanding children and the impact the world around them has on their self-esteem. Self-esteem is something we are all dealing with every day with everyone we meet or work with, and more importantly within ourselves. It is the essence of our successes, interactions, relationships, abilities, goals, our view of ourselves, and the world around us. Self-esteem cannot be neglected because if it is, life can seem like a dispiriting struggle.

Self-esteem is the vital ingredient for success and happiness in our lives. When we have it we feel good about ourselves, we feel calm, confident and in control and everything is possible. It seems that a sudden loss of self-esteem is common to everyone. We all need to know what we can do to 'lift ourselves up again' when things go wrong and we lose our self-belief.

Good self-esteem is priceless and utterly vital for happiness and success. Feeling good about ourselves makes our world more exciting.

Throughout this booklet there are activity pages you can use with your child. Have some fun!

CREATING A GOOD ENVIRONMENT

Anyone who has a significant impact on a child's life, eg. family members, friends, childminders and teachers, must take responsibility for building self-esteem. We refer to these people as 'esteem builders'. They must create an environment that will help self-esteem develop.

Home environments that help to build self-esteem can usually be described as:

- Caring.
- Supportive.
- Secure.
- Warm.
- Non-threatening.
- Trusting.
- Comfortable.
- Non-judgemental.
- Accepting.
- Encouraging.
- Inviting.
- Positive.
- Listening.

How many of these qualities does your child experiences day to day? These things seem simple but are crucial to us all.

Research has shown that there are three critical elements that are common to the homes of children who have a good healthy self-esteem:

- Their backgrounds provided experiences that express respect, concern and acceptance. As children they were accepted for their strengths and capabilities as well as for their limitations. It is clearly 'love with no strings attached'.

- The less permissive their parent's lifestyle, resulted in children developing a higher self-esteem. There were clearly defined limits, standards and expectations and as a result, children felt secure.

- Their families functioned with a high degree of democracy. As children they were encouraged to have their own ideas and opinions as part of family discussions and decisions, even those that deviated from their parents.

The factors that are most effective in building self-esteem and self-images are those that allow children to:

- Live amongst people who provide a sense of warmth, love and care.
- Have a degree of security that allows them to grow and try new things without an overriding concern about failure.
- Know they are respected as individuals.
- Be encouraged and to have ideas and opinions.
- Recognise that there are clear and definite limits within the environment.
- Understand rules and standards that are reasonably and consistently enforced.
- Have a chance to succeed at their own levels.
- Feel accepted with 'no strings' attached.

In order for children to cope with the ups and downs that life brings it is crucial for significant people in the child's life to create good solid roots and give positive messages which the child can rely on when the going gets tough. Good foundations help us to bounce back.

When we consider the human rights of every child, we know that they all deserved to feel loved and significant to anyone we would class as an esteem builder. Children also need guidance and boundaries that help them to understand how to behave. We should aim to provide a family life that is high in warmth and low in criticism. However, research shows that many children do not live in a warm and caring environment, but one of criticism and blame. This can result in them having negative feelings about themselves and others.

Consider which type of family environment you are providing for your child. Are you providing high warmth or high criticism? Do not forget, nobody is perfect and we all make mistakes sometimes.

The quality of communication between parent and child regularly emerges as a link to levels of self-esteem. We should always be aware that children need messages that tell them that even if they are wrong, they are still OK as a person. Consider which of the following four options sum up the messages between you and your child?

I am ok **You are ok**	I am not ok You are ok
I am ok You are not ok	I am not ok You are not ok

The one to aim for is 'I am ok and you are ok'.

A very large factor of a child's self-esteem is the external forces in their lives. Repeated patterns or experiences, whether they are positive or negative, help mould self-opinions. Whether or not another individual can change a child's current self-esteem depends on how significant the individual is to the child.

An esteem builder is someone who has the ability to change a child's self-opinion for the better and who has an influence on the child. It will be someone who the child sees as worthy, important or significant in order to be effective. It is important for the esteem builder to gain a child's trust and respect and they should invite and nurture healthy, good feelings in the child. Remember, it is the child's parents that have the biggest impact on their learning.

UNDERSTANDING CHILDREN'S BEHAVIOUR

When children are really playing up it is common to find ourselves dealing with all behaviour with equal anger. It feels very much as if they do everything deliberately to annoy us. The reality is not quite true. The following are three areas of behaviour that all children present at some time or other. These headings are referred to in the book 'Dare to Discipline' by James Dobson.

1.   Childish Irresponsibilities.

        Children do all manner of silly things. They spill drinks, dirty clean clothes, forget what they have been told or get into arguments over what appear to be very unimportant things. You can send your child off to school looking beautiful but when they return they look scruffy, are covered in mud and have scuffed their shoes. Children always seem to find the muddiest place to play! Most of us have experienced those mealtimes when they are perhaps cutting a sausage and the knife slips and food shoots off the plate in many directions. It is amazing how many times you can put clean clothes on your child and within moments they have spilt something down them. Our natural reaction is 'What did you do that for?' The truth is, they did not do it on purpose. It would be interesting to remember how many times we, as grown-ups, have done something equally as silly. Have you ever accidentally broken something or misplaced your keys just as you are leaving the house?

        Children do not do these silly things deliberately to annoy us. Of course, these silly things need to be handled, but they need to be put into context with the more serious aspects of behaviour. Consider how you might feel if you were told off for something you did not mean to do? How does this affect your self-esteem?

2.   Behaviour Linked with Development.

        A six-year-old child was observed taking a toddler up some steps in a large shop. The six-year-old was getting very angry with the toddler for being so slow. The toddler was still at the stage of putting two feet on the same step and had not acquired the skill of passing easily from one step to another. She was not being naughty, but was unable to fulfil what was being asked of her. Other examples include the young child who may not be using a potty properly, or a toddler who is messy when eating. For an older child, it might be that they have been given instructions to look after the younger ones while you pop out for a short time. You arrive back to chaos. Even though they are older, they might not have yet gained adult skills in handling young children. The younger ones may well have played up deliberately to get the older child into trouble. Many parents find the two-year-old stage hard work because of the vast amount of learning that the child is experiencing. It is very hard to keep up with them! The adult must be aware of the amount of learning going on and celebrate it rather than make it a problem. From now on we will call this stage "the tremendous two's" and see it as our chance to provide the right sort of learning.

        We can easily fall into the trap of comparing our children with those of our friends, forgetting that children develop at different speeds. No behaviour linked to a child's development is done deliberately to annoy us.

Consider the stage of development your child is at presently and the things you need to teach, help with, and be more patient about? Remember how it feels when you are told off for something you do not know how to do. A good example is during teenage years when there are so many physical changes happening. We forget that hormones make people moody.

3. Challenge to Parent's Authority.

This is the more serious aspect of our children's behaviour. Defiance and stubbornness come into this category. In this situation, the child is usually very aware of what they are doing. Most of us have experienced this – we give an instruction that we expect to be carried out and our child takes a stand against us and says 'No!'

It may be that we have instructed them not to do something and they deliberately do precisely what we have told them not to. The challenge is, 'What are you going to do about it?' This is indeed the more serious aspect of behaviour. Many of us have backed away from this challenge only to find that our child challenges more and more frequently. We need to face this challenge and we need to set down boundaries or learn to regret it for the remainder of our child-rearing years.

Just imagine what life will be like if our children refuse to do anything we say. They will strive to control us and treat us with contempt in the process. The truth of the matter is they want and need us to control them. Without this control, children feel insecure and afraid of their own power; this is when they become unmanageable. It feels as if they are hyperactive when, in fact, they want someone stronger than them to take control. When we do take control they will still challenge and test us, but they need to do this. It is part of exploring and testing out life and also making sure that we are still able to handle them.

We all need security and will find ways to challenge those closest to us to see what they are made of and if they mean what they say. Challenging behaviour is a healthy response and a way of learning about the world. If children are not allowed to test out our world they may not grow to be all they are meant to be.

ANGELA'S WORD

When Angela was very young, aged two or three or so,
Her mother and her father taught her never to say NO.
They taught her that she must agree with everything they said,
And if she didn't, she was spanked and sent upstairs to bed.

So Angela grew up to be a most agreeable child;
She was never angry and she was never wild;
She always shared, she always cared, she never picked a fight,
And no matter what her parents said, she thought that they were right.

Angela the Angel did very well at school
And, as you might imagine she followed every rule,
Her teachers said she was so well-bred, but so quiet and so good,
And how Angela felt inside... they never understood.

Angela had lots of friends who liked her for her smile,
They knew she was the kind of girl who'd go the extra mile;
And even when she had a cold and really needed rest,
When someone asked her if she'd help she always answered yes.

When Angela was thirty-three, she was a lawyer's wife.
She had a home and family, and a nice suburban life.
She had a little girl of four and a little boy of nine,
And if someone asked her how she felt she always answered 'fine.'

But one cold night near Christmastime when her family were in bed,
She lay awake... as awful thoughts went spinning through her head,
She didn't know why, and she didn't know how, but she wanted her life to end;
So she begged whoever put her here to take her back again.

And then she heard, from deep inside, A voice that was soft and low;
It only said one single word and the word it said was....NO!.
From that moment on, Angela knew exactly what she had to do.
Her life depended on that word, so this is what her loved ones heard;

NO, I just don't want to;
NO, I don't agree;
NO, that's yours to handle;
NO, that's wrong for me;
NO, I wanted something else;
NO, that hurt a lot!
NO, I'm tired, and NO, I'm busy,
And NO, I'd rather not!

Well, her family found it shocking, even her friends reacted with surprise;
But Angela was different you could see it in her eyes;
And they've held no meek submission since that night three years ago
When Angela the Angel got permission to say NO.

Today Angela's a person first, then a mother and a wife.
She knows where she begins and ends, she has a separate life.
She has talents and ambitions, she has feelings, needs and goals.
She has money in the bank and an opinion at the polls.

And to her boy and girl she says, 'It's nice when we agree:
But if you can't say NO, you'll never grow to be all you're meant to be.
Because I know I'm sometimes wrong and because I love you so,
You'll always be my angels even when you tell me NO.'

Poem by Barbara K. Bassett

UNDERSTANDING HOW SELF-ESTEEM DEVELOPS

The development of a child can be broken down into six areas. All children develop at different rates. It can be very confusing to determine the cognitive stage of development that the child has attained, very often this is judged by the child's size, age or physical ability alone, when in fact emotionally or socially he/she may be functioning at a lower or higher level. We have to help the child to succeed by setting goals that are achievable and not by expecting the child to perform at a level they have not yet learned or developed into. The six areas of development are known as:

S P I C E S

Social   Physical   Intellectual   Cultural   Emotion   Spiritual
or
Self-Esteem

In order for a child to reach their full potential in all aspects of their development, attention must be given to self-esteem as the one single recipe for achievement that will be individual for every child. Children need to feel special and unique, and every stage of their development should be recognised and encouraged.

Unfortunately, many children are surrounded by stronger messages of disapproval than of acceptance, which will influence their view of themselves. These children receive negative comments, predictions of future failures, no recognition of current successes, and withdrawals of affection.

When a child has the concept of low self-worth, their development cannot progress to its fullest potential. Research shows that children who have high self-esteem become winners.

TEENAGE DEVELOPMENT

Understanding the way that teenagers develop can be very intricate. In fact we all develop at different rates and with different life experiences that influence the way we mature, our understandings, our view of the world, others and ourselves.

As children grow up there are six main areas of development to consider. These areas do not stop developing when children become teenagers or indeed adults; we are learning and developing all the time. The six main areas of development come into the following basic categories:

Social Development - This is how we interact with others and our skills in communication. Social development can often appear to take a backward step during teenage years alongside the changes that are going on in some of the other categories. Remember that when a teenager just uses one-word answers they have not regressed developmentally, it is just them going through the normal stages of development. Peer group, music and credible influences are most important at this stage.

Physical Development -	We are all aware of the vast physical changes that happen to children during their teenage years, some are visible and others are not. These physical changes can monopolise and effect the way a teenager thinks about themselves. Hormonal changes make us moody and lacking in vitality.
Intellectual Development -	During a time when there are so many other developmental changes going on for a teenager, they are also going through the most vital part of their educational learning. This can create enormous stress for some teenagers. This area also includes the development of other life skills both educational and practical.
Cultural Development -	This category is not just about race, religion or our heritage, it also includes awareness of the values and beliefs within daily life, particularly within the family and the impacts that these have on the teenager as an individual person. An example of this might be that if we are brought up in a family where ridicule and sarcasm are normal, we might grow up to feel stupid and undervalued.
Emotional Development -	This covers areas such as caring, coping and empathy. Our emotional responses to different situations e.g. bereavement, divorce, successes and failures, and the way in which we learn to feel and cope with them fits into this category. Emotions during teenage years can be very acute whilst going through the teenage stages. Just a spot on the face can be all it takes to send a teenager into an emotional crisis.
Spiritual Development -	This might appear to be related to religion but is primarily linked to the teenager's view of themselves and their view of the world. It is about self-esteem. 'Who am I? What or who do I want to be? What is it all about?' This is the category that links with self-esteem and their view of themselves and others. From an early age we gain an understanding of how we impact on those around us, and most importantly how they impact on us. This determines what and how we think about ourselves.

SOME SIGNS OF LOW SELF-ESTEEM

These are some examples of the things people say if they have low self-esteem. Look out for them.

Permanent Talk	*"Things always go wrong for me, I never have any luck"*.
Global Talk	*"I've always been lazy"*.
Internal (Self Blame)	*"I always ruin everything"* (exclusively my fault).

Temporary Talk	*"This won't last I'm just waiting for things to go wrong".*
Specific Talk	*"The only good thing in my life is my music".*
External Talk	*"Yes I got in the team so the others must have been really bad"* (credit given externally).

CHANGES IN BEHAVIOUR

When a child is going through a difficult stage of development or there are things in their life that are affecting his/her self-esteem, one of the first signs to look out for is them being critical of themselves and their parents. This often leads to defensiveness and a tendency to flare up quickly. It is wise not to respond in the same way to this type of behaviour, but to remember that you are responsible for demonstrating to your child how to cope and become resilient.

Children may also display how they feel through their body language and how they talk to us. They may appear rude or sarcastic and have an "I can't be bothered" attitude. If parents do not understand that this behaviour is directly linked to self-esteem, they might give out the wrong message to the child, for example, "Don't come to me for help", "Don't ask me for money" or "You won't have any friends if you talk to people like that".

The danger is that the child may turn to someone or something else for a sense of security or self-esteem, and parents need to be aware that it might not always be the right place.

UNDERSTANDING THE 5 COMPONENTS OF SELF-ESTEEM

Michelle Borba, an American researcher refers to self-esteem under the following 5 components. They help us to gain a clearer view of how self-esteem develops. As a child grows and has more life experiences, their inner picture of themselves expands. The inner picture consists of all the descriptions an individual attaches to him/herself and is called self-concept.

1. SENSE OF SECURITY
    This is a feeling of certainty. It involves feeling comfortable and safe, knowing what is expected, being able to depend on individuals and situations, and understanding rules and limits.

2. SENSE OF BELONGING
    This is a feeling of connection and acceptance particularly in relationships that are considered important. Feeling approved of, appreciated and respected.

3. SENSE OF SELFHOOD
    This is a feeling of individuality. It gives us a sense of who we are based on how we view ourselves and how we believe others view us.

4.   SENSE OF PURPOSE
This is a feeling of motivation and satisfaction in life. Being able to set realistic and achievable goals and being able to voice an opinion and make choices.

5.   SENSE OF ACCOMPLISHMENT
This is a feeling of success and achievement in things regarded as important or valuable. Being able to acknowledge our strengths and accept our limitations.

PERSONAL QUALITIES NEEDED TO BUILD SELF-ESTEEM

It is important that parents understand the things they can do to help develop their child's self-esteem. Parents who wish to improve their child's self-esteem should posses the following qualities:

- A sincere interest and concern for the child.
- A desire to build a trusting relationship and be someone who is both reliable and trustworthy.
- A willingness to make the effort and to take the time to help their child feel better about themselves.
- A real belief that the child's self-esteem can change and the ability to communicate that to her/him with confidence.
- A willingness to review one's own self-picture periodically being aware that the esteem builder's role is vital.
- A genuine recognition of the positive qualities of each individual.
- A personal rapport so the child feels significant to their parent/esteem builder.
- A willingness to 'open up' to children and share genuine qualities and experiences with them.

ADULT BEHAVIOUR THAT PROMOTES HIGH SELF-ESTEEM IN CHILDREN

- Give your child time, listen to them and try to understand how they feel.
- Let them know you love them as often as you can.
- Offer choices sometimes such as what they would like for dinner.
- Encourage them in things they do well.
- Give responsibilities that they can do easily, such as helping with the washing up or carrying things to the kitchen.
- Talk with them about anything they are finding difficult and make some sensible suggestions to help them.
- Give regular praise.
- Tell them you trust them and demonstrate this by giving them appropriate levels of responsibility.
- Celebrate their achievements.
- Demonstrate appropriate behaviour, e.g. manners, respect, calmness etc.
- Define appropriate boundaries.

1. SENSE OF SECURITY

DEFINITION
This is a feeling of certainty. It involves feeling comfortable and safe, knowing what is expected, being able to depend on individuals and situations, and understanding rules and limits.

SIGNS OF LOW SECURITY
- Avoids certain situations or places.
- Withdraws from close physical contact even with known persons.
- Distrusts others.
- Avoids or hesitates forming close personal attachments.
- Exhibits stress or anxiety symptoms (nail biting, thumb sucking, hair twirling, teeth grinding, shaking, rocking, crying) without apparent reason.
- Challenges authority.
- Displays excessive and/or unfounded fears.
- Is uncomfortable with new experiences.
- Lacks knowledge of who can be counted on.

SIGNS OF HIGH SECURITY
- Knows who to count on and trust.
- Generally feels safe and secure, therefore risks separating from trusted sources for brief periods.
- Displays few symptoms of stress and anxiety.
- Has formed a trusting, personal relationship with a significant other.
- Is comfortable with close physical contact from known persons.
- Handles change and spontaneity with relative ease.

THE MAIN THINGS TO REMEMBER
- Build a trusting relationship.
- Set reasonable limits and rules that are consistently enforced.
- Create a positive and caring environment.

BUILDING SECURITY
Building security is the first step towards developing a child's self-esteem – it is the most essential component. It helps the child develop a strong healthy view of themselves. Children must feel safe and assured in their environment in order to grow.

Another aspect of being a good esteem builder is to give praise where deserved. We know it has significant effects when dealing with challenging behaviour but it is also a powerful technique for enhancing self-esteem. Different methods of praise are outlined below:

Deserved   Children know if their praise is deserved, be sincere.

Immediate   Praise on the spot, it is more effective than after the event.

Behaviour centred	To begin with, praise what the child did rather than aim the praise directly at them, otherwise they will become suspicious and feel your are not being genuine.
One to one	Start off low key and try not to embarrass them, verbally praise or send a text message (if old enough to have their own phone) or leave a note.
Specific	Let the child know exactly what was done well.
Repeated	Praise frequently to help the message to become internalised. Repeated praise is effective. The more the child hears it, the more they will believe it.
Spontaneous	A spontaneous comment can be very effective.

List of People I Can Depend On

People you can trust are people you can count on.
They are there when you need them, can keep a secret
and can always be depended upon to help.
Who are the people you can trust?

Directions:
Make a list of people you can trust. Under each name write
why the person is so special and why you can count on them.

1. _____

   _____

   _____

2. _____

   _____

   _____

3. _____

   _____

   _____

4. _____

   _____

   _____

5. _____

   _____

   _____

...and who can depend on me?

Child's Name _____   *Date* _____

ECOMAP

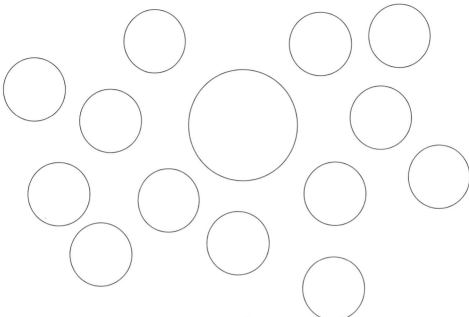

- Place the child's name in centre circle.

- Identify important people in the child's life, e.g. parents, siblings, teachers, doctor, friends, family members etc. and draw circles as needed.

- Draw lines between the circles where connections exist, using the different types of lines to indicate the nature of the link or relationship.

———— = strong link

– – – – = weak link

········ = stressful link

Remember, sometimes we want someone in the middle circle with us to help us out when we are nervous or lacking in confidence.

Who would you put there with you? _____

Child's Name _____ *Date* _____

2.SENSE OF BELONGING

DEFINITION
This is a feeling of connection and acceptance particularly in relationships that are considered important. Feeling approved of, appreciated and respected.

SIGNS OF A LOW SENSE OF BELONGING
- Has difficulty initiating and maintaining friendships.
- Connects with objects rather than with people.
- Is easily influenced by others.
- Isolates themselves from the group, appears to be lonely.
- Is uncomfortable working in group settings which may result in behaviours such as: withdrawal, reticence, bullying, showing off, being silly, monopolising, being uncooperative etc.
- Ridicules or rejects others, being insensitive to their emotions or needs.
- Feels that others do not value him/her.
- Brags and boasts excessively to gain approval.
- Relies on adult companionship as sole source of affiliation.
- Is seldom sought out by others.

SIGNS OF A HIGH SENSE OF BELONGING
- Understands the concept of friendship and initiates new relationships.
- Shows sensitivity and compassion towards others.
- Demonstrates the ability to co-operate and share.
- Is comfortable in group settings.
- Easily achieves peer acceptance and is sought out by others.
- Demonstrates appropriate social skills.
- Feels valued by others.

THE MAIN THINGS TO REMEMBER
- Promote inclusion and acceptance within the family or with friends.
- Provide opportunities to discover interests, capabilities and backgrounds.
- Increase awareness of and skills in friendship making.
- Encourage peer approval and support.

BUILDING A SENSE OF BELONGING
This component of self-esteem is about the recognition received in relation to others. Interpersonal relationships in our lives are vital, we all need to feel close to another human being, in particular those who we consider to be important and significant to us. When we have a good attachment or bond with those closest to us, and are shown respect and approval, we gain a good sense of belonging.

Friendships have an enormous influence on our feelings of self, so clearly affiliation is an important building block towards positive esteem. Peers are an essential part of social development that cannot be fulfilled by family experiences alone.

The following aspects are crucial to developing a high sense of affiliation.

- Peer interaction helps to shape a young person's self-perception or identity.
- Acknowledge your child's individual uniqueness. Do not compare children as it can make your child feel that they are not good enough.
- As we win some acceptances and experience a few rejections, we build significant views about ourselves.
- Group experiences will develop a sense of belonging.
- Early negative experiences will need to be balanced out by friends, family members, teachers, and significant others in the child's life.
- Helping to share and co-operate will develop the child's ability to form meaningful, trusting and honest relationships.
- Early attachments and bonds are good building blocks towards being able to gain a sense of belonging.
- Build good healthy caring relationships around the child.
- Even through the hard times the parent should always let their child know that they will be there for them.

Think of ways you can be a friend to someone. Write each friendly deed in a different section of the Friendship Wheel.

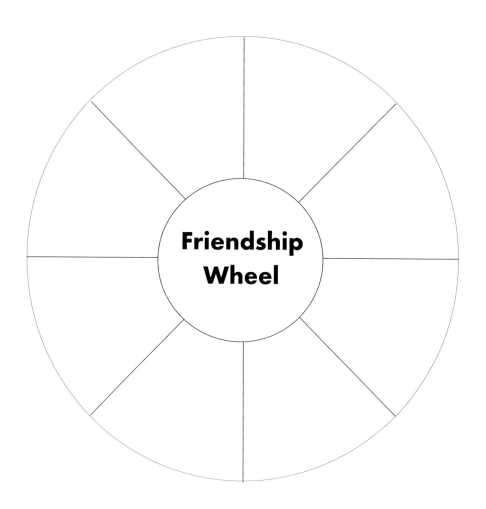

Friendship Wheel

Child's Name _____   *Date* _____

SPECIAL PERSON FOR THE DAY ACTIVITY PAGE

Let us pretend that today is your special day. Everyone is going to be especially friendly to you today. They want to know what you would like them to do so that they can be sure to get it right. What will you tell them?

I like it when friends and family...

_____

_____

_____

_____

_____

It is not friendly to...

_____

_____

_____

_____

_____

_____

Child's Name _____   *Date* _____

3. SENSE OF SELFHOOD

DEFINITION
This is a feeling of individuality. It gives us a sense of who we are, based on how we view ourselves and how we believe others view us.

SIGNS OF LOW SELFHOOD
- Frequently uses negative statements about themselves and others.
- Embarrasses easily and is oversensitive to criticism.
- Lacks in confidence and presentation so may appear shy and withdrawn. Will not want to highlight their skills, and dislikes being in the spotlight.
- Is dependent on adults and is anxious to please them.
- Is uncomfortable and embarrassed by praise and consequently denies, undermines or disregards their achievements.
- Conforms or mimics others, and is unwilling to express themselves in their own way or risk being different.
- May seek acknowledgement for negative characteristics.
- Is misinformed regarding roles, attributes or physical characteristics.
- Dresses in extremes, either to attract attention or to cover up the body.

SIGNS OF HIGH SELFHOOD
- Handles most activities with ease.
- Expresses uniqueness and individuality, risks being different.
- Has an accurate self-description in terms of physical characteristics, capabilities, roles and attitudes.
- Generally makes positive statements about themselves and others.
- Identifies and expresses emotions appropriately.

THE MAIN THINGS TO REMEMBER
- Reinforce more accurate self-descriptions.
- Provide opportunities to discover the things that will influence.
- Build an awareness of unique qualities.
- Enhance the ability to identify and express emotions and attitudes.
- Acknowledge the way that advertising and the media affects us all.

BUILDING SELFHOOD
When a solid framework of security has been achieved you can concentrate on others aspects. In this component we are addressing the child's perception of themselves, and the way they describe themselves.

The self-description a child has about themselves may or may not be accurate, but for the child it can appear to be very accurate. It is helpful to give genuine and honest comments and you may need to do so for a long period before the child will begin believing you, particularly if someone has convinced them they are no good or unattractive. Low self-image will have an impact on many aspects of a child's life.

Below is a list we of important things that we should remember when building self-esteem:

- The way we describe a child will have a massive impact on their self-image.
- Provide the child with a healthy lifestyle and diet to prevent illness and promote high energy levels.
- A child forms their physical self-image very early on in life.
- There are numerous outside influences that affect our self-image such as TV adverts.
- A child's concept of attractiveness may have a powerful impact on their social relationships throughout their life.
- Research has shown that children who have a negative image of their body are likely to have negative feelings about themselves as a person.
- Many of us need a more realistic view of our personal characteristics and traits, remember we all tend to be less likely to accept compliments than criticism, work hard to accept praise.
- We need to build on our strengths and form an accurate self-picture with which we can feel comfortable and even proud.

THINGS I LIKE ABOUT ME   ACTIVITY PAGE

Think about all the things that you like about yourself and that you would not want to change.

Some things I really like about me are...

Child's Name ------------------------------------ *Date* ------------------------

There are lots of words that I can use to describe people.

I can describe how they look (e.g. tall, short, blue eyes, curly hair etc).

I can describe what they are like (e.g. happy, thoughtful, kind etc).

Child's Name ------------------------------- *Date* -------------------------

4. SENSE OF PURPOSE

DEFINITION
This is a feeling of motivation and satisfaction in life. Being able to set realistic and achievable goals, being able to voice an opinion and make choices, and willing to take responsibility for the consequences of our actions.

SIGNS OF A LOW SENSE OF PURPOSE
- Lacks motivation and initiative.
- Cannot see alternatives and solutions.
- Feels powerless, therefore may exhibit attention seeking behaviours such as whining or squabbling to gain control.
- Appears aimless and without direction.
- Rarely succeeds due to expectations being set too high and unachievable.
- Is over dependent on others and feels incapable of making suggestions or influencing other people.
- Will avoid taking responsibility for his/her own actions and therefore is quick to blame others.
- Indecisive and will avoid making decisions preferring someone else to do it.

INDICATORS OF HIGH SENSE OF PURPOSE
- Appears purposeful with a clear sense of direction.
- Plays alone for periods and does not always need adult direction.
- Takes responsibility for his/her own actions and recognises the consequences.
- Can make choices and has an opinion which can be voiced.
- Seeks alternative solutions to problems.
- Sets achievable and realistic goals.
- Can begin to gauge personal limitations and learn from mistakes.

THE MAIN THINGS TO REMEMBER
- Encourage children to have an opinion and make choices. Teach how to consider options and alternatives and think through the impact of the decisions we make.
- Take time to point out how much progress has been made in your child's life. Talk about things they used to do when they were little and celebrate their learning and progress constantly.
- Support your child's choices providing they do not put him/her in danger, one of the best ways to learn is by experience, so be there to support things if they do not work out.
- Teach steps to successful goal setting.

BUILDING A SENSE OF PURPOSE
It is amazing how children turn out to be what we encourage them to be. People who have a high self-esteem generally feel self-motivated and have a clear sense of direction. Mostly because they have a good sense of their aims and have intentions to achieve them. Achieving enhances self-esteem and supports the notion that we can reach out and make plans, have hopes for the future that we can succeed in meeting. Achievement energises us and so we can go on to set more goals.

The responses we receive to our personal hopes and aspirations will affect our belief in ourselves. These responses will determine whether or not the risks are worth taking. With constant encouragement, realistic aims and resources, even the occasional knock back can be refocused into a positive outcome or opportunity to redirect. Encouragement is the real key to building a child's self-esteem in this area.

USING OUR IMAGINATION TO HELP US   ACTIVITY PAGE

Have you ever made up a story in your head?   Imagined that you saw something that was not really there? Heard a noise and imagined it was something scary? Have you ever remembered the taste or feel of something that is not actually in front of you?   Do you ever imagine that you are somewhere else? Doing something different?

These are all images and they come from your imagination. We all have the power of imagination and we can all use our imagination to help ourselves, sort out problems, feel good, cope with troubles when they come along and to help us to do the things we want to do.

Use your imagination in a helpful way.

Child's Name ---------------------------------------   *Date* -----------------------------

OVERCOMING FEELINGS

Have you ever worried about something that has not happened yet? What did your body feel like?
Tick the feelings that you get when you are worried.

Butterflies in my tummy ☐   Heart beats faster ☐

Headache ☐   Fidget a lot ☐

Feel sick ☐   Can not think clearly ☐

Feel like crying ☐   Wobbly knees ☐

Have you ever got excited about something long before it happened? What did your body feel like then?

_____

_____

_____

_____

_____

_____

_____

Your imagination can make your body feel different things. Sometimes this is good, but sometimes this is not useful for you. Sometimes you might need to change what you are imagining so you can feel better.

Imagine that!

Child's Name _____   Date _____

THINGS I AM WORKING ON

All through life we are learning new things and often getting better at some of the things we can already do or we already know about. Lets imagine that on prize-giving day at the 'School for Magicians' they also give awards for the things that you are working on.

These are things that are a bit difficult for you at the moment so you are learning a bit more about them or practicing them regularly so they become easier for you to achieve.

Think of five things you are working on and write them here.

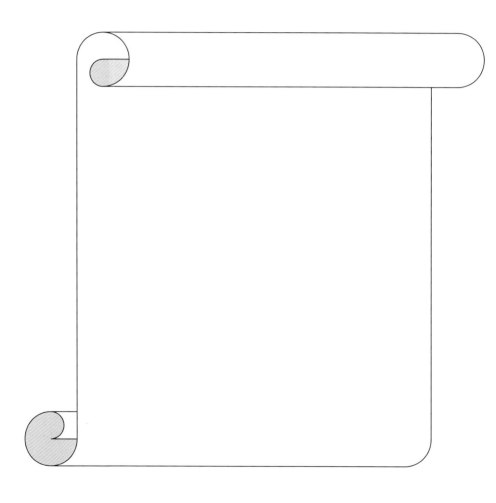

Child's Name _____   Date _____

5. SENSE OF ACCOMPLISHMENT

DEFINITION
This is a feeling of success and achievement in things regarded as important or valuable. Being able to acknowledge our strengths and accept our limitations.

SIGNS OF A LOW SENSE OF ACCOMPLISHMENT
- Is reluctant to contribute ideas or opinions.
- Is unwilling to take risks.
- Acts as if helpless and is dependent in areas where he/she can or should be competent.
- Acts out in areas where he/she feels competent by displaying frustration, withdrawal, lack of participation, resisting, defying, day dreaming, or cheating.
- Does not attempt many tasks because of over riding fear of failure or insecurity.
- Displays an 'I can't' attitude and does not try.
- Is a poor loser, magnifies any loss or displays poor sportsmanship.
- Makes negative comments about their achievements, often leaving things discredited.

SIGNS OF A HIGH SENSE OF ACCOMPLISHMENT
- Seeks out challenges and takes risks.
- Accepts limitations and uses mistakes as a learning tool.
- Is aware of strengths and positive characteristics.
- Generally feels successful at things deemed important.
- Eagerly shares opinions and ideas.
- Displays good sportsmanship and can handle defeat.
- Recognises their accomplishments and achievements, but is conscious not to brag or be arrogant about them.

THE MAIN THINGS TO REMEMBER
- Provide opportunities to increase awareness of competencies and strengths.
- Enjoyment is often worth more than achievement.
- Allow your child to make mistakes and let them know that nobody is perfect.
- Teach the importance of self-praise and of accepting praise for things we do well.

BUILDING A SENSE OF ACCOMPLISHMENT
Children get a sense of accomplishment following frequent successes. Children who have a good sense of achieving will concentrate on their own individual strengths rather than their weaknesses. They will know that their contributions are important and are valued.

We want children to be winners and have some resilience to cope with life's stresses. Do not expect too much, it is better to aim a little lower and achieve rather than set unrealistic targets.

Now lets imagine that every person at the 'School for Magicians' gets a gold medal for something that they are really brilliant at. What will your gold medal be for?

Draw a picture or write about something that you are really brilliant at.

Child's Name _____   *Date* _____

Here are some examples of certificates you could give your child as an acknowledgement of their good behaviour.

Congratulations

You have worked so hard
and it has not gone unnoticed.
I want you to know how much…

…I admire you!

From _____ *Date* _____

Special Person
Award

You have done a thoughtful and kind deed.
I want you to know your are a …

…very special person!

From _____ *Date* _____

Child's Name _____   Date _____

When someone has done something well or really tried hard, they might be praised for it. The good thing about praise is that it can happen at any time and for lots of different reasons.

To praise someone means: ....

....

I can praise people by: ....

....

When people praise me I feel: ....

....

Today I praised someone for : ....

....

Something I would like to be praised for is:

....

....

....

Certificate of praise

we like your ★ smile!

"JUST BECAUSE I CAN!"

Parents give up on their children usually because of a lack of energy, ability and skills to know what to do next, or because they have problems of their own. Children can get an incorrect view of themselves. In some families where the child has all the 'say' e.g. they decide what is for tea, what to watch on TV, or even what time everyone goes to bed, the child grows up thinking they have a right to make all of those decisions. Being too grown up before their time can make a child believe they have a right to make all the decisions. Do not be scared to parent your child in a loving, fair and developmentally appropriate way.

WHAT TO DO WITH WORRIES   ACTIVITY PAGE

Imagine that you could post your worries into a worry box.

What do you think should happen to them then?
Where would they go?
Would anyone look at them? If so, who would it be?
What would they do with them?
Draw or write about what happens.

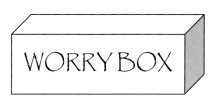

Child's Name _____   *Date* _____

QUESTIONNAIRE

Complete this questionnaire on your own. Give each section considerable thought. Discover areas within yourself that you wish to work on.

SECURITY
1. Consider who or what you have in your life that you can trust 'no matter what' and that you feel completely at ease with.
2. How do you view changes that occur in your life?
   - I find change difficult, I prefer what I know.
   - Quite well.
   - I see change as a challenge and positive experience.
3. List any new experiences you may have had in the last year.
4. Do you enjoy your job? What aspects do you like? Why are you in this line of work?

SELFHOOD
1. Describe your personality.
2. What do you like most about yourself?
3. List some of the nicest things that anyone has said to you?
   How do you feel about these comments? Are they true? Do you believe them yourself?
4. What are you good at?
5. Are you good at expressing emotions? Do you over react?
   - Sometimes.
   - Always.
   - Never.
6. Is there a particular person that this reaction happens around? Ask yourself why.
7. Make a list of things that are really special about yourself.

BELONGING
1. What qualities do others see in you?
2. Who are your longest standing friends and how long have you known them?
3. Name one friend or person you have met recently.
4. Do you get anxious about meeting new people?
5. How do you enjoy your leisure time?
   - By yourself.
   - With family.
   - With friends.
6. Do you allow yourself enough leisure time?
7. How often do you put others before yourself?
   - Often.
   - Always.
   - Sometimes.
   - Never.

PURPOSE
1. When taking part in group activities e.g. work related or hobbies, do you:
   - Take the lead.

- Withdraw or hold back.
- Take part when it feels right for you.

2. Are you good at making decisions? Do you believe in your gut feelings? Do you take too long and miss the boat?
3. Think of one good decision you have made recently.
4. How good are you at your job?
   - Exceptional.
   - Very good.
   - Good.
   - Fair.
   - Not very good.
5. What particular qualities or skills do you bring to your job?
6. What do you see yourself doing or what would you like to do in the next few years?
7. How often does your opinion influence others?
   - Always.
   - Sometimes.
   - Never.

ACCOMPLISHMENT

1. Think of something that you suggested that turned out well.
2. Does your life seem to present difficulties?
   - Often.
   - Sometimes.
   - Never.
3. Do you seem to attract difficulties?
4. What are you good at?
5. What do you want to develop for yourself?
6. List your personal achievements over the last year. It may be something you are proud of.
7. If you enter a competition how would you describe yourself?
   - A poor loser.
   - A good sport.
   - Very competitive.
   - I never usually win anything.
8. When confronted with a very difficult task would you:
   - Give up easily.
   - Give it a good try.
   - Keep going until you completed it.

When you have completed this questionnaire reflect on your responses and decide if there is anything that you could work on. Are you happy with your responses? Build plans for change step by step.

Work on building your own self-esteem. It helps to have a high self-esteem when we are helping others.

LOOKING AFTER OUR OWN SELF-ESTEEM

There are many excellent books on self-esteem for adults. These are just a few 'key' points to take into consideration.

- Make time for yourself. You are important.
- Set regular short-term goals as well as long-term goals. Make sure they are realistic and attainable.
- Make sure any self-criticism is constructive not destructive.
- Be ready to accept constructive criticism from others and to cope with unjustified criticism in an assertive way.
- Own your feelings. Do not assume that others know what you are feeling.
- Use 'I' statements, such as 'I am angry' not 'You make me angry'.
- Be able to forgive yourself for past mistakes.
- Acknowledge your successes and reward yourself.
- Be proud of who you are and what you achieve.
- Accept sincere compliments and praise from others.
- Try to eliminate self-defeating phrases from your speech.
- Learn the skill of being your own friend.
- Learn to like yourself.

A BRIEF STORY

A Simple Gesture By John W. Schlatter

Mark was walking home from school one day when he noticed that the boy ahead of him had tripped and dropped all the books he was carrying, along with two sweaters, a baseball bat, a glove and a small tape recorder. Mark knelt down and helped the boy pick up the scattered articles. Since they were going the same way, he helped to carry part of the burden. As they walked, Mark discovered the boy's name was Bill, that he loved video games, baseball and history, that he was having a lot of trouble with his other subjects and that he had just broken up with his girlfriend.

Mark went home after dropping Bill at his house. They continued to see each other around school, had lunch together once or twice, then both graduated from junior high school. They ended up in the same high school, where they had brief contact over the years. Finally the long-awaited senior year came. Three weeks before graduation, Bill asked Mark if they could talk.

Bill reminded him of the day years ago when they had first met. "Do you ever wonder why I was carrying so many things home that day?" asked Bill. "You see, I cleaned out my locker because I didn't want to leave a mess for anyone else. I had stored away some of my mother's sleeping pills and I was going home to commit suicide. But after we spent some time together talking and laughing, I realised that if I had killed myself, I would have missed that time and so many others that might follow. So you see, Mark, when you picked up my books that day, you did a lot more. You saved my life."

Remember, 'A child's life is like a piece of paper on which every passer by leaves a mark'.

SMILING IS INFECTIOUS

Smiling is infectious,
you catch it like the flu.
When someone smiled at me today,
I started smiling too.

I passed around the corner,
and someone saw my grin.
When he smiled I realised,
I'd passed it onto him.

I thought about that smile,
then I realised its worth.
A single smile just like mine,
could travel the earth.

So, if you feel a smile begin,
don't leave it undetected.
Lets start an epidemic quick,
and get the world infected!

Unknown Author.

ACKNOWLEDGEMENTS

Compiled by Joy Osborn and Sue Stead
Administrative support by Laynie Osborn and Carrie Prosser-Shaw

Provides professional training, advice and consultation to those
working with children and families in any capacity.

Joy Osborn and Sue Stead
Company Directors
Future Childcare Training Ltd
P.O. Box 4388
Rugby
Warwickshire
CV21 9DN

Tel & Fax: 024 7654 5500
Email: info@FutureChildcareTraining.com
Website: www.FutureChildcareTraining.com

taking your parenting to the next level...

Future Childcare Training Ltd has other books for parents to purchase. To order copies of any of our parenting books please visit our website and click on the bookshop page for further details:
www.FutureChildcareTraining.com

A Parent's Guide to Building Self-Esteem

A Parent's Guide to Handling Children's Behaviour

A Parent's Guide to Handling Teenage Behaviour

taking your parenting to the next level...